Try Not To Laugh

Challenge

300 Jokes for Kids that are Funny, Silly, and Interactive Fun the Whole Family Will Love

Jokes For Kids Volume 1

Smile Zone

ISBN: 9781711167497

Table of Contents

Introduction

From the chuckles we get in the highly anticipated Popsicle stick punchline to the excited trading on the playground during recess, jokes play an important and formative role in the everyday lives of children. As a parent, we know you want to be a part of that. But knowing the best way to interact with your children isn't always obvious. A shared, familiar sense of humor could be the bridge you need to best help your child grow.

A good sense of humor is important for the healthy mental and social development of children. It helps them not only get along better with their peers but also assess new and different situations open-mindedly and creatively. This is why Smile Zone is excited to bring you this cover to cover chuckle-fest. We crafted a book chocked full of fun and funny jokes of all sorts.

We want to help you not only play a positive role in your child's development but to bond with your child as well. So, crack open these jokes in the car, on the beach, or anywhere you can use a good laugh. This book can guarantee giggles and good times for all, but that's just an added benefit on top of all the good you are doing for your family.

No one should underestimate the value of a great laugh shared among friends and family so read alone to share later or read below to take our try not to laugh challenge with those close to you. No matter what you do, we have no doubt good times will be had by all.

The Rules

For 2 Players Or 2 Teams of Players

Rules for Players: Each player takes turns reading one joke from the book. They do not have to read the jokes in order and may choose any joke within the book. If the listener laughs then the reader gets a point. Then the book is given to the other player and it is their turn to read. Sighing or eyerolling doesn't count and neither does smiling, but any form of laughter is worth 1 point, be they giggles, chuckles, or peals. The first player to 7 points wins.

Rules for teams: The rules are the same for two teams of players except that each person has to take a turn reading. The teams score one point for each person who laughs. So, if there is two people on a team you get two points if they both laugh, but only one if one of them laughs. Also, with teams, you need 7 points for each player to win. With two people on a team, you need 14 points to win, 21 with 3 people, and so on.

Remember to be fair and always admit if you laugh, games with arguments are no fun at all. And the most important rule is to laugh as much as you can!

Chapter One

People Jokes

1. What is a waiter's favorite sport?

Tennis, because he knows how to serve!

2. Why did the farmer ride his horse to town?

It was too heavy to carry!

3. How do sailors get their clothes clean?

They throw them overboard and they wash ashore!

4. What do you call a dentist who doesn't like tea?

Denis!

5. When does a joke become a "dad" joke?

When the punchline is a parent!

6. How much does it cost a pirate to get his ears pierced?

About a buck an ear!

7. How does a scientist freshen her breath?

With experi-mints!

8. What's a pirate's favorite letter?

Not Arrrrrrrrr, his first love is the C!

9. Where do mermaids look for jobs?

The kelp-wanted section!

10. Why did the golfer wear two pairs of pants?

In case he got a hole in one!

11. What did the fisherman say to the magician?

Pick a cod, any cod!

12. Why couldn't the pirate play cards?

Because he was sitting on the deck!

13. Why couldn't the athlete listen to her music?

Because she broke the record!

14. What did the tooth say to the dentist as she was leaving?

Fill me in when you get back!

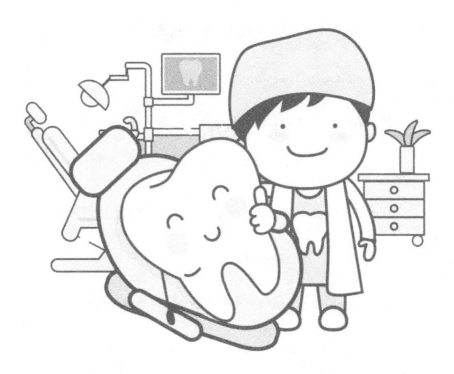

15. What kind of car does a farmer drive?

A corn-vertable!

16. How did the farmer mend his pants?

With cabbage patches!

17. Patient: Doctor, sometimes I feel like I'm invisible.

Doctor: Who said that?

18. Who made King Arthur's round table?

Sir-Cumference!

19. Why did the man run around his bed?

Because he was trying to catch up on his sleep!

20. What do you call two guys hanging up a curtain?

Kurt and Rod!

21. Did you hear about the two guys who stole a calendar?

They each got six months!

22. What do postal workers do when they're mad?

They stamp their feet!

23. Guy in a library walks up to the librarian and says, "I'll have a cheeseburger and fries, please."

Librarian responds, "Sir, you know you're in a library, right?"

Guy says, "Oh, sorry. [in a whisper] I'll have a cheeseburger and fries, please."

24. What is an astronaut's favorite key on the keyboard?

The space bar!

25. What nails do carpenters hate to hit?

Fingernails!

26. How did the butcher introduce his wife?

Meet Patty!

27. Why was the worker fired from the car assembly line?

She was caught taking a brake!

28. What's the IT person's favorite button?

F5 because it's so refreshing!

29. Why did the old lady fall in the well?

Because she didn't see that well!

30. Why did grandma put wheels on her rocking chair?

So she could rock 'n' roll!

31. Doctor, doctor! I feel like a pack of cards!

I'll deal with you later...

32. I told my doctor that I broke my arm in two places.

He told me to stop going to those places!

33. Who says sticks and stones may break my bones, but words will never hurt me?

A guy who has never been hit with a dictionary!

34. Did you hear about the guy who fell into an upholstery machine?

He's fully recovered!

35. What do you call a really good plumber?

A drain surgeon!

Chapter Two

School Jokes

1. Why did the clock go to the principal's office?

For tocking too much!

2. How do you get straight A's?

By using a ruler!

3. Why did the teacher carry birdseed?

She had a parrot-teacher conference!

4. In which school do you learn how to make ice cream?

Sunday School!

5. How did the music teacher get locked in the classroom?

He couldn't find the right key!

6. Why did the clock in the cafeteria run slow?

It always went back four seconds!

7. What is a butterfly's favorite subject at school?

Mothematics!

8. Teacher: Give a sentence beginning with "I"

Student: I is...

Teacher: Stop there, you need to begin with "I am."

Student: Okay...I am the ninth letter of the alphabet.

9. What school do you have to drop out of to graduate from?

Parachute school!

10. What did the little boy's mom say when he asked her to buy him shoes for gym?

"Tell Jim to buy his own shoes."

11. Why don't you see giraffes in elementary school?

Because they're all in High School!

12. Why are kindergarten teachers so valuable?

They can make little things count!

13. How many books can you put into an empty backpack?

One. After that, it's not empty!

14. Where do math teachers go on vacation?

Times Square!

15. Who's in charge of the pencil box?

The ruler.

Chapter Three

Animal Jokes

1. What do you call a cold dog sitting on a bunny?

A chili dog on a bun!

2. What do you call a dog magician?

A labracadabrador!

3. What do you call a cow that eats your grass?

A lawn moo-er!

4. What's the biggest moth in the world?

A mammoth!

5. How do fish go into business?

They start on a small scale!

6. What do you call a cow with no legs?

Ground beef!

7. What is the most musical part of a fish?

The scales!

8. Why do hummingbirds hum?

They forgot the words!

9. What do you get if you cross a serpent and a trumpet?

A snake in the brass!

10. What did the Dalmatian say after lunch?

That hit the spot!

11. What do you call a duck that gets all A's?

A wise quacker!

12. Why does a seagull fly over the sea?

Because if it flew over the bay, it would be a baygull!

13. Why don't elephants chew gum?

They do, just not in public!

14. Why do bees have sticky hair?

Because they use a honeycomb!

15. Why aren't dogs good dancers?

They have two left feet!

16. What do you call a deer with no eyes?

No-I-Deer!

17. Why do porcupines always win the game?

They have the most points!

18. Why do you never see elephants hiding in trees?

Because they're so good at it!

19. What is the worst kind of key to unlock a door with?

A monkey!

20. What do you call an ape that loves potato chips?

A chip-panzee!

21. What do you call a cow with three legs?

Lean beef!

22. What do porcupines say when they kiss?

Ouch!

23. What's a cow's favorite holiday?

Moo-morial day!

24. Where do sheep go to get haircuts?

The baa-baa shop!

25. How do cats bake cakes?

From scratch!

26. Why wouldn't the shrimp share his treasure?

Because he was a little shellfish!

27. What do you give a sick bird?

A tweetment!

28. What do cows read?

CATTLE-logs!

29. Why do tigers have stripes?

So they don't get spotted!

30. What animal is always the life of the party?

The owl, they're a real hoot!

31. Why do fish live in salt water?

Because pepper makes them sneeze!

32. How do you fit more pigs on your farm?

Build a sty-scraper!

33. What do you call a cow that won't give milk?

A milk dud!

34. What animals are most often found in legal documents?

Seals!

35. What is animal is always out of bounds?

An exhausted kangaroo!

36. What animal has more lives than a cat?

Frogs, they croak every night!

37. What kind of bird works at a construction site?

The crane!

38. What do you call a dead parrot?

A polygon!

39. What do you call a funny chicken?

A comedi-hen!

40. Where did the school of kittens go for their field trip?

To the mewseum!

41. Have you ever seen a catfish?

No. How did he hold the rod and reel?

42. How can you best raise a baby dinosaur?

With a crane!

43. Why was the Stegosaurus such a good volleyball player?

Because he could really spike the ball!

44. What did the dog say when he sat on sandpaper?

Ruff!

45. Why are dogs like phones?

Because they have collar IDs!

46. Why are elephants so wrinkled?

They're too big to iron!

47. What is gray and blue and very big?

An elephant holding its breath!

48. When does a horse talk?

Whinney wants to!

49. What do you call a rabbit who is angry over getting burnt?

A hot cross bun!

50. What did the beaver say to the tree?

It's been nice gnawing you!

51. What goes tick-woof and woof-tock?

A watchdog!

52. What does a spider's bride wear?

A webbing dress!

53. Where do cows go for entertainment?

The mooooo-vies!

54. What creature is smarter than a talking parrot?

A spelling bee!

55. What animal needs to wear a wig?

A bald eagle!

56. How do you know if there's an elephant under your bed?

Your nose touches the ceiling!

57. What do you call an alligator in a vest?

An investigator!

58. Where newborn cows eat?

The calf-eteria!

59. Why did the pig go into the kitchen?

He felt like bakin!

60. What do you get when you cross a tiger and a lamb?

A striped sweater!

61. Why did the whale cross the ocean?

To get to the other tide!

62. What's a dog's favorite instrument?

A trombone!

63. Which animal has fur but barely uses it?

A bear!

64. What does a koala look for in furniture store?

Koality stuff!

65. How do you start a communication with a fish?

You drop him a line!

66. Why does a woodpecker have a beak?

So they don't smash their head against the tree!

67. Cute little bunny comes in a pharmacy and asks if they have carrot ice cream.

"No. This is a pharmacy. We don't sell ice cream."

Bunny leaves. But it comes back the next day and again asks, "Do you have carrot ice cream?"

"No, Bunny! This is a pharmacy. We don't sell ice cream!"

Bunny leaves – but comes again the next day. And the next day, and so on, until after about two weeks, the pharmacist caves in and personally gets carrot ice cream for the next time the bunny comes.

The bunny does come, and again asks, "Do you have carrot ice cream?"

"Today, Bunny, today we do!" smiles the pharmacist.

The bunny says: "Well then don't eat it. It tastes horrible!"

68. Why do hens lay eggs?

Because if they were throwing them, they'd break!

69. Where do bulls leave their fliers?

On a bull-etin board!

70. What were the Snake's last words?

Oh drat, I bit my tongue!

71. How do you catch a whole school of fish?

With bookworms!

72. What do geese take for their allergies?

Anti-hissssss-tamines!

73. Why should you never trust a pig with a secret?

'Cause it's bound to squeal!

74. Why couldn't the pony sing?

She was a little hoarse!

75. Why do ducks make great detectives?

They always quack the case!

76. How do you turn a bear into a B?

Take away its ear!

77. What do you get when you cross-breed a skunk and a vegetable?

A smellery!

78. Why has a giraffe got a long neck?

Because his feet stink!

79. Who granted the fish a wish?

The fairy codmother!

80. What type of bull is the cutest?

An adora-bull!

81. What do you call an exploding monkey?

A Bab-boom!

82. What happened when the owl lost her voice?

She didn't give a hoot!

83. How do you help an injured pig?

Call a hambulance!

84. What do you call a snake on a building site?

A boa constructor!

85. Did you hear about the two silk worms that had a race?

It ended in a tie!

86. How do bears keep cool?

They use bear-conditioning!

87. What kind of bands do whales like?

Orca-stras!

88. What do you call lending money to a bison?

A buff-a-loan!

89. What has four legs and says oom?

A cow walking backwards!

90. What do you call an elephant in a phone booth?

Stuck!

91. Why do cows wear bells?

Because their horns don't work!

92. What is the easiest way to count a herd of cattle?

With a cowculator!

93. How many skunks does it take to make a big stink?

A phew!

94. What do you call a mommy cow that just had a calf?

Decalfinated!

95. What has 4 wheels, gives milk, and eats grass?

A cow on a skateboard!

96. What do you give a pig with a rash?

Oinkment!

97. What pine has the longest needles?

A porcupine!

98. What do you call snake with no clothes on?

Snaked!

99. What do you call a dinosaur at the rodeo?

Tyrannosaurus Tex!

100. Where do horses live?

In the neigh-borhood!

101. What do frogs like to eat in the summer?

Hopsicles!

102. Why don't oysters share their pearls?

Because they're shell-fish!

103. Why are A's like flowers?

Because bees come after them!

104. Why wouldn't they let the butterfly into the dance?

Because it was a mothball!

105. What do you call a bird in winter?

A brrrr-d!

106. What's a camel's favorite beverage?

Camel-mile tea!

107. Why aren't koalas actual bears?

They don't meet the koalafications!

108. What do you call a bee that can't make up its mind?

A maybe!

109. What do you get when you cross a dog and an antenna?

A Golden Receiver!

110. What happened to the dog that swallowed a firefly?

It barked with de-light!

111. What do you get when you cross a cow and a duck?

Milk and quackers!

112. What kind of egg did the bad chicken lay?

A deviled egg!

113. What kind of key has feathers?

A turkey!

114. What's black and white, black and white, black and white, and green?

Three skunks fighting over a pickle!

115. My dog used to chase people on a bike a lot.

It got so bad, finally I had to take his bike away!

116. Can a kangaroo jump higher than the Empire State Building?

Of course! The Empire State Building can't jump!

117. What do you get when you crossbreed a mail pigeon and a parrot?

A mail pigeon who stops to ask for directions!

Chapter Four

Nature Jokes

1. When is the moon the heaviest?

When it's full!

2. How do you throw a party in space?

You planet!

3. What is brown, hairy, and wears sunglasses?

A coconut on vacation!

4. What kind of shorts do clouds wear?

Thunderwear!

5. How do you cut a wave in half?

You use a sea saw!

6. What is worse than raining cats and dogs?

Hailing taxis!

7. What do you call a funny lil' mountain?

Hill-arious!

8. What did the big flower say to the little flower?

Hi, bud!

9. What is the only tree that serves in the military?

The infant-tree!

10. What's brown and sticky?

A stick!

11. What sits at the bottom of the ocean and shakes?

A nervous wreck!

12. What is the best time of year to jump on a trampoline?

Spring time!

13. Why is it impossible to trust atoms?

They make up everything!

14. Which runs faster, hot or cold water?

Hot, because you can catch cold!

15. What happens when you wear a snow suit inside?

It melts all over the carpet!

16. What kind of music do planets sing?

Neptunes!

17. What do planets like to read?

Comet books!

18. What is a tree's least favorite month?

Sep-timber!

19. What do you call a fast fungus?

A mush-vroom!

Chapter Five

Knock-Knock Jokes

1. Knock Knock!

Who's there?

Broccoli.

Broccoli who?

Broccoli doesn't have a last name, silly!

2. Knock Knock!

Who's there?

Cash.

Cash who?

I knew you were a nut!

3. Knock knock!

Who's there?

Dishes.

Dishes who?

Dishes me, who are you?

4. Knock Knock!

Who's there?

Cow says.

Cow says who?

NOOOOOO! A cow says moo!

5. Knock, knock!

Who's there?

Cargo.

Cargo, who?

Car go, "Beep beep, vroom, vroom!"

6. Knock, knock!

Who's there?

Catsup.

Catsup who?

Your cat's up a tree and won't come down!

7. Knock, knock!

Who's there?

Radio.

Radio, who?

Radio-not, here I come!

8. Knock, knock!

Who's there?

Lettuce.

Lettuce who?

Lettuce in and you'll find out!

9. Knock, knock!

Who's there?

Woo.

Woo who?

Don't get so excited, it's just a joke!

10. Knock, knock!

Who's there?

Theodore.

Theodore who?

Theodore is stuck and it won't open!

11. Knock, knock!

Who's there?

Doris.

Doris who?

Doris locked, that's why I'm knocking!

12. Knock Knock!

Who's there?

Iva.

Iva who?

Iva sore hand from knocking!

13. Knock Knock!

Who's there?

Duane.

Duane who?

Duane the tub, I'm Drowning!

14. Knock, knock!

Who's there?

Canoe.

Canoe who?

Canoe help me with my homework?

15. Knock, knock!

Who's there?

Anee.

Anee, who?

Anee one you like!

16. Knock, Knock!

Who's there?

Stopwatch.

Stopwatch who?

Stopwatch you're doing and open this door!

17. Knock, knock!

Who's there?

Needle.

Needle who?

Needle little money for the movies!

18. Knock, knock!

Who's there?

A herd.

A herd who?

A herd you were home, so I came over!

19. Knock, knock!

Who's there?

Adore.

Adore who?

Adore is between us. Open up!

20. Knock, knock!

Who's there?

Ivor.

Ivor who?

Ivor you let me in or I`ll climb through the window.

21. Knock, knock!

Who's there?

Aida.

Aida who?

Aida sandwich for lunch today!

22. Knock, knock!

Who's there?

Ben.

Ben who?

Ben knocking For 10 minutes!

23. Knock, knock!

Who's there?

Tank.

Tank who?

Your welcome!

24. Knock, knock!

Who's there?

Althea.

Althea who?

Althea later alligator!

25. Knock, knock!

Who's there?

Viper.

Viper who?

Viper nose, it's running!

26. Knock, knock!

Who's there?

Spell.

Spell who?

Okay, okay: W. H. O.

27. Knock, knock!

Who's there?

Mikey.

Mikey who?

Mikey doesn't work so help me out, would you?

28. Knock, knock!

Who's there?

You left the door open!

Chapter Six

Food Jokes

1. What do you call a berry that exploded?

A blew-berry!

2. What did the skeleton order for dinner?

Spare ribs!

3. What do you call a sad strawberry?

A blueberry!

4. What is fast, loud, and crunchy?

A rocket chip!

5. What did one plate say to the other plate?

Dinner is on me!

6. How does a cucumber become a pickle?

It goes through a jarring experience!

7. What do you do if you get peanut butter on your doorknob?

Use a door jam!

8. How does a train eat?

It goes chew chew!

9. Why do we put candles on the top of a birthday cake?

Because it's too hard to put them on the bottom!

10. How did the egg get up the mountain?

It scrambled up!

11. Why did Billy go out with a prune?

Because he couldn't find a date!

12. What is black, white, green, and bumpy?

A pickle wearing a tuxedo!

13. What are twins' favorite fruit?

Pears!

14. Which fruit is a vampire's favorite?

Neck-tarine!

15. Where do hamburgers go to dance?

They go to the meat-ball!

16. What type of bagel can fly?

A plain bagel!

17. What does a sea monster like to eat?

Fish and ships!

18. What vegetables do sailors hate the most?

Leeks!

19. Why did the man get fired from the orange juice factory?

He couldn't concentrate!

20. Some lettuce, an egg, and a faucet had a race. What was the result?

The lettuce came in ahead, the egg got beat, and the faucet is still running!

21. What does the toast wear to bed?

Jammies!

22. How do you make a rock float?

Put it in a glass with some ice cream and root beer!

23. What's the difference between mashed potatoes and pea soup?

Anyone can mash potatoes!

24. What's a dog's favorite food for breakfast?

Pooched eggs!

25. What do cows like to put on their sandwiches?

MOOstard!

26. Why did the coffee go to the police?

It got mugged!

27. What kind of tea you drink with the Queen?

Royal tea!

28. What's the most colorful kind of berry?

A crayon-berry!

29. Why did the sea monster eat five ships that were carrying potatoes?

No one can eat just one potato ship!

Chapter Seven

Jokes About Anything and Everything

1. What is a balloon's least favorite kind of music?

Pop music!

2. What was stolen from the music store?

The lute!

3. What did the left eye say to the right eye?

Between us, something smells!

4. Why don't robots have brothers?

Because they only have trans-sisters!

5. What musical instrument is found in the bathroom?

A tuba toothpaste!

6. Why was the broom running late?

It over-swept!

7. What part of the car is the laziest?

The wheels, because they are always tired!

8. Can February March?

No, but April May!

9. Why did the computer go to the dentist?

It had a blue tooth!

10. What did the finger say to thumb?

I'm in glove with you!

11. Did you hear about the kidnapping in the park?

They woke him up!

12. Which is the longest word in the dictionary?

"Smiles," because there are miles between each "s."

13. Did you hear the joke about the roof?

Never mind, it's over your head!

14. Why did the picture go to jail?

Because it was framed!

15. Why do bicycles fall over?

Because they are two-tired!

16. Why was the belt arrested?

Because it held up some pants!

17. Why don't traffic lights ever go swimming?

Because they take too long to change!

18. Has your tooth stopped hurting yet?

I don't know, the dentist kept it!

19. Where does a boat go when it's sick?

To the dock!

20. What happened when the wheel was invented?

It caused a revolution!

21. What is the hardest part about skydiving?

The ground!

22. Why did the toilet paper roll down the hill?

To get to the bottom!

23. What is big, green, and plays a lot of tricks?

Prank-enstein!

24. How do locomotives hear?

Through the engineers!

25. What kind of boat goes around a castle?

A Moat-or boat!

26. Which part of the car has the most fun?

The WHEEEEEls!

27. What's the books favorite make up.

Lip glossary!

28. What do you get when you cross a snowman with a vampire?

Frostbite!

29.What's the difference between a poorly dressed man on a tricycle and a well-dressed man on a bicycle?

Attire!

30. Why is tennis such a loud game?

Because each player raises a racket!

31. What has four wheels and flies?

A garbage truck!

32. How can you tell that a train just went by?

It left its tracks!

33. Where are cars most likely to get flat tires?

At forks in the road!

34. What is the world's longest punctuation mark?

The hundred yard dash!

35. What do envelopes say when you lick them?

Nothing, it shuts them up!

36. Why is b always cool?

Because it's always near ac!

37. What's a monster's favorite game?

Swallow the leader!

38. Did you hear about the guy who was crushed by books?

He's only got his shelf to blame!

39 What gives you the power to walk through a wall?

A door!

40. Why do people hate Russian nesting dolls?

They're so full of themselves!

41. Have you heard about corduroy pillows?

They're making headlines!

42. What are green, red, orange, purple, blue, and yellow?

Colors!

43. Where do books hide when they're scared?

Under the covers!

44. Why shouldn't you be slow while getting on the bus?

Because you wanna Bus-to-move!

45. What is green, fuzzy, and if it fell out of a tree would kill you?

A Pool table!

46. What's orange and sounds like a parrot?

A carrot!

47. Why don't matches play baseball?

Because they are out after just one strike!

48. I wanna hang a map of the world in my house. Then I'm gonna put pins into all the locations that I've traveled to.

But first, I'm going to have to travel to the top two corners of the map so it won't fall down!

49. Last night, I had a dream that I was a muffler.

I woke up exhausted!

50. I couldn't figure out why the baseball kept getting larger.

Then it hit me!

51. I ate a clock yesterday,

it was very time consuming!

52. Two windmills are standing in a wind farm.

One asks, "What's your favorite kind of music?"

The other says, "I'm a big metal fan."

53. Paul: I have good news and bad news. Which do you want to hear first?

Michael: The good news.

Paul: The good news is that I have no bad news.

54. Why was everyone so tired on April 1st?

They had just finished a March of 31 days!

55. What is the smartest part of the eye?

The pupil!

56. What streets do ghosts haunt?

Dead ends!

57. Why did the chicken cross the road?

Because the road was too long to go around!

58. Does it take longer to run from 1st base to 2nd, or from 2nd to 3rd?

From 2nd to 3rd because there's a shortstop in the middle.

Conclusion

And there you have the most hilarious jokes we could find. For more family fun and entertainment, make sure to check out other titles available from Smile Zone.

CPSIA information can be obtained
at www.ICGtesting.com
Printed in the USA
BVHW042238060520
579337BV00009B/551

9 781711 167497